AF255808

The Visionaries

The Visionaries

ANASTASIA PATSOURI

RESOURCE *Publications* · Eugene, Oregon

THE VISIONARIES

Resource Publications
An Imprint of Wipf and Stock Publishers
199 W. 8th Ave., Suite 3
Eugene, OR 97401

www.wipfandstock.com

PAPERBACK ISBN: 978-1-6667-6418-5
HARDCOVER ISBN: 978-1-6667-6419-2
EBOOK ISBN: 978-1-6667-6420-8

01/03/23

*Dedicated to my father Stratis,
my mother Anna-Maria and
my sister Eugenia*

CONTENTS

CONTENTS

OMICRON

Gorgeous blue glow
My wings of flow
Somewhere did I read
Butterflies exist

In poisonous amounts
Gifting true discounts
Your enemy is fear
Trusting your own deer

Tigers are apart
Swamps alert
Misty bless
Secrets dress

Stripes of lust
Treasure own crush
Wounds of touch
Sound of crouch

Folding and expanding
Contracting deconstructing
Programms deinstall
Freedom reinstall

Your virtue be it self
Communities unrest
Fire wishing seldom
Dancing immer welcome

STREETS

Picking up flowers
During rush hours
Hustle and beauty
Gardens urban duty

Babel's Tower
Blow up power
Keys to unlock
Hearts never block

Freedom to seek
Divine sleek
Coining the joy
Virtue employ

Traumas be flowers
Bouquets of pain
Darkness domain
Colors of rain

Till white spins it all
You, whirling dervish
Starting to cherish
Light slides out

Rays of wisdom
This is your kingdom
Purpose is freedom
Act now in still-dome

POLITICS

Under my skin
Reside spirits
Particles of air
Bubbles of care

Flying around
Red crown
Color is right
You are alive

Sweet nurse
Kissing soul
Removing riddles
Dancing needles

Left ain't forget
That side gives more
Stronger veins
System drains

History's battle
Human natures rattle
Who's gonna win
Empathy is a twin

You, black dot
Ain't exist alone
White font defines you
Dualisms refine you

MINDPEACE

Blow a kiss
Doctors' bliss
Knew the lyrics
Forgot the freaks

Dance the waste
Babylonias case
Enjoy the system
Cares for freedom

Control your powers
Take care of your showers
Boarding in peace
Paper cranes

Eagles drains
Fix your brains
Straight up
Live love laugh

SEAWALK

World is crazy
And today you are a bit lazy
Swim in peace
Sway in style

Mirrors of sea
Finally arrived
To rescue the mermaid
No winds today

Only clean sky
Is the world spinning
Asked Michelle
Yes it does

I replied firmly
As always
Making sure
Calm peace and love

Govern the globe

WETTER

Books of destiny
Shared efthimy
Epiphany of love
Little blue dove

Systems of creation
Lost liberation
Collage me twice
I show you a slice

Of what real life means
Welcome to queens
The district of Heart Chor
Relieving down dog

Chopping those sticks
Bamboo kiss
Wind of change
East west one chain

ATHENS

Teach me
Yellow skyline
Acropolis die-line
Colors of wisdom

Athenian kingdom
Ancient aura
Modern traffic
Red lights cartographic

Urban mystery
Moneys misery
Rocky paths
Marble laughs

Riding bikes
Helmet dislikes
Ice cream heavens
Coffees burdens

Loud and proud
Royal gypsy
Olympic queen
Fantasies redeem

THE REST

Learning how to rest
Never ending test
Repeating those mistakes
'Til you pull those breaks

Somebody once whispered
Sleep, the little brother of death
You got trapped and enslaved
Paying souls unpaid depth

Previous lives previous lies
Keep exercising those tries
Place your ego out of the box
Allow your soul feel unorthodox

Wisdom is pain
Just make it rain
Dancing outside
Residing inside

Feel centered
Get rid of regrets
Confidence forgiveness
Mean love to your in-ness

Allow the mess
It's ok, distress
You know after all
Caress and success
Circulate the stress

Keep moving
Keep talking
Stars are all ears

Universal connection
Global affection

Energy to ride
Communities align
Foster your goals
Ghost all of ya fears
It's where you pull up the gears

Enjoy today
Cause you heard from them
That sleep is indeed
Needed and wised
lil brother of death

EYELASHES

Lioness in exile
In front of you I bow
The power of tunes is now
North light to seek

Blessings to redeem
Beam swim
Eternal sunshine molly
Breathing rays of grace

What is your final race?
Attractions like in atoms
Electrones plus and minus
The one who ate your lust

Is the one you now trust
Demons sleepy girl
Picturing in glass
What is your own class

Eyelashes falling
Morpheus hug wide open
Compression to remove
Life lasting to fuel

Watch out it ain't unnerving
Your virtue shall be serving

BRIDGE MOMENT

You used to be a spy
Now you make me cry
Bridges of emotions
resolve atrocious

War of gender
Kissing tender
Delay of clay
Building up sway

Allow me to ask you
It's cold outside
Naked I stand
Trusting the hang

Clang of believers
Patient beevers
Crews of anomalies
Scarify all gondoliers

Perception of time
Expanding the lust
Missing the years
Truly bright tears

Joy saudade
Dancing forró
This life is a ho
Unpaid bills

Cherish all thrills

MORNING WORKOUT

Shower your dreams
Cut off streams
That scare your thrills
Allow moments

Facial recognition
Sleeps in your conscious
Dance out all fears
Rhythm and tears

Craniotomy of music
New bones explored
They say it's the third
Pulsation of lust

Breathing your heart
Troubadour of band
Your thoughts are expanding
Allow them to feel

How wild intelligence
Can drive you mad
Outrageous I vibrate
Signals be sending

Neurones tender out
My wishes work out
Body recreation
Soul salvation

CRISIS

I wonder how to fit
Your wisdom
In my kingdom

Your false alarm
Be steady and calm
Rejuvenate it all

Until there's no one left
To cherish your emotion
What I call true devotion

Endeavors are your flavors
Watch out what you try
Spicy life be challenging

Fire was what trebling
Gave you so much lust
To live life's trust

Adults in the room
Children in the heart
Don't worry or be sorry

Unified we stand
All sorrows to split
Feeling ones guilt

Until you explode

Crisis to manage

Courage is your package

EUROZONE 2011

Interrogation is affection
Process liberation
Psychologists you trust
Friends of old lust

Duty is creation
Own sensation
Liberty of wisdom
Unite dual kingdom

When adults cry out
And kids smile in
Then the world keeps round
Turning and profound

When kids cry in
And adults scream out
Crisis exists
Half or even none

Call old nun
Salaries of Labor
Recession is depression
Economies catastrophication

Until comes classification
Identity's salvation
To release rivers of joy
Unslave all kids ahoy

Make peace for sake of love
Blue ground white dove

ALEX

Fox of the night
Speakers up tight
In front of court
Wisdom your sword

Electro Jazzy Afro
Asking «τι είναι αυτό»
Fathers be your angels
Enlarge secret hangers

Dry out all your sorrows
Monarchy's deep horrors
Release rivers of joy
Humor, life's a toy

Your hands of creation
Fragile sweet vibration
Stronger immer holding me
Securing vivid knowing me

Boxing out all fears
Kicking out long tears
Running fast thin deers
Lions vowels and careers

Prince of unrest
Universe's strength your test
Private own nest
Music's common caress

Undress, call your freedom
Brains cold kingdom
Swimming sea of lust
Growing pure trust

LILLY

Lady of the wolves
Ecstatic is your song
While you reach that point
Of joy and emotion

True devotion
Photography your language
Lenses are caressing
Your aura's spirit

Lady of the wolves
Barefoot brujita
Dancing chiquita
Under the moonlight

Rivers and waterfalls
Colombian wonders
They all bow
To your charming glow

Allow them to kiss
Eternal bliss
Charisma your currency
Freedom your urgency

Huge heart
Beauties attack
Your eyes of wisdom
Your souls kingdom

JULIE

Bambi of the Alps
Smoothening scalps
Imagination is your key
Creation how you flee

Élysée your old home
Museums' new dome
Cameras are ready
Films be steady

Beauty of the mountains
Climbing up above
Fountain of love
Your soul's white dove

Ceramics your wisdom
Breaking up kingdom
Freedom to redeem
Glory unforeseen

VICTOR

Ministry of public offense
Spreading love nonsense stress
War of freedom
Sexual kingdom

Taurus to lead
Labyrinths to seek
Innovation is creation
Border your frustration

Diplomacy your key
International erosion
Personal explosion
Allow me to admit

Deep diving is the hit
Spot my reaction
Natural contraction
Until I explode

Nuclear sensation
Attraction like in atoms
Electrons plus and minus
Who taught you all such lust

Stop buying own trust

ERUPTION

Your touch
My chests lust
Fire under the skin
Volcanos bright sins

I'm luring up your spirit
I'm lingering to hear it
I want to endure
Heavens to ensure

Your kiss is approaching
My body is now crouching
Skins left alone to dance
Passion in trance

Projections on the wall
Scenes of the past
Hunting us at last
Escaping now together

Its us who choose
Which movie each time
To play is a ray
Let the sun come in

Its us who choose
Which movie to play
Each time is a ray
Let the sun come in

Shadows to elude
Clarity now nude
Moments of caress
Keep away distress

Ride on those colors
All the shades of lust
Volcanic is the touch
Lets try a deep match

GODS PLAYING

Torso of Venus
Chest of Ares
While Hera and Zeus
Enjoy such heavens

Olympian drains
Feeling no pains
For lovers who hide
Seek and fly

Delivering flairy
Atmosphere ahead
Mountain goddess
Sitting up straight

Evoking and provoking
Waves of lust
Figuring own trust
Long strange dreams

Lasting steady dusting
Caressing what we call
Temples of love

Venus of affection
Ares liberation

PLANET VENUS

Ultraviolet wavelengths
Venus naked eye caress
Planet earth sisterhood
Beauty and love
Symbols above

Ultraviolet wavelengths
Solar System flavors
Planetary emotion
True sensual devotion

Venus in fairs
Up for all flares
Atmospheric gesture
Magnetic runaway

Interplanetary space
Eternal grace
Orbiting my rivers
Of joy and shivers

Terrestrial megaplace
Embrace the chase
Life on Venus
Our own genus

ANDROMEDA

Queen of Addis Ababa
Andromeda's story
Desacralized faith
Poseidon's huge laith

Lapping waves
Cetus grave
Waiting for the beauty
Nereid's duty

To shine bright star
Galaxies afar
Perseus saved her
Eros starting to occur

Ethiopian love
Athenian dove
Lighting north sky
Death defy

ARTEMIS

Diana of the Versailles
Hunting me down
Under the sunlight
Blue caravan your home

To truly exist
Between the gods
Of love and affection
Own liberation

Animal kingdom
Natures wisdom
Wilderness to seek
Rebirth to redeem

Lunar celebration
Children formation
Virginity of fame
Sudden blame

Artemis be thoughtful
Wholesome I pray
Newborn clay
To shape my future

My life's suture
Arrows in the sky
This is how we fly
Eternal freedom

Olympus kingdom

LOOSE EMOTION

Loose emotion
True devotion
Dancing we fly
Limit is the sky

Comfortable
Feeling the way out
Reasons blurry
Please don't hurry

Loose emotion
Loving me slow motion
We're all in promotion
Endless chance

Until you explode
Something on the road
I should know
Stars make it how

Bliss a kiss
Im telling you
Bad since '93

HEART CHOR

That ecstasy I feel
When you all just surround me
Vibration vocalizing
My sorrows transatlantic
Transforming outta space

Moon shines above my Tenors
We bow out of caress
That night was a success

My Altos shaking boodies
Maestro rolling fire
Sopranos keep me high
Sensations curing joy
My Base ain't forget
That grounding voice to lead

The luck I feel around you
No words can describe
The hug of wings you offer
Fly me further deep inside

To truly understand
How joy takes all colors
Embracing them is learning

The luck I feel around you
No words can describe

Eternal love comes singing
For all different species
Our jungle is a treasure
Kingdom of Heart Chor

THERAPY

Cancel culture
Me too
Tell me now what
Am I supposed to do

Rough times
Thin lines
Thick streets
Need skins

Dignity is gone
Standing all alone
Communities vibrating
My mind contracepting

6 weeks of therapy
6 months of despair
Learning how to care
Growing is the legacy

Pain is the lecture
Exam me sir I know
The lyrics of by heart
Melodies of freedom

Layers of lucidum
Lucid dreams of aid
Fears to combat
True calms to arhat

An angel calling stop
Your chest overburning
Your mind now turning
Perspectives to embrace

Slowing down aint a flaw
She is waving with her paw
Ignoring is audacity
Exploring is Felicity

True self to arrive
Avoid to deplore
That journey of self care
No moment you forget

That ride aint a sprint
A marathon is life.

WHERE THE CRAWDADS SING

Social workers unfolding
My soul's trembling
There's no wrong young lady
That's what we sing

Water flows into the sky
Where horizons kiss
Coastal bliss
Marsh full of light

Prisons consider
Learning from the wild
Protecting yourself
Ever shifting

From summer to fall
Am I here at all
Life changing in a second
Turn on the music

The only constant
In nature is change

ALEXAKI

Bambi true porn
Completely now torn
Affection pure cotton
Souls crave from their bottom

"Attraction like in atoms
Electrons plus and minus
Who ate all of your lust
Where is your tender touch"

I sang for you on stage
Audience high erected
My love resurrected
For what was 4 years

Freely running deers
Your wisdom stays my kingdom
Prism of different lives
White helpful silent lies

Unspoken was the truth
No real words my tooth
Silent sealed eyes
Black magic full of cries

Tears my emotion
Fears your devotion
Trust is a lust
Ride ain't crush

Dying is no option
Stock your brains auction
Selling and reselling
Your souls unveiling

Invisible your hands
Holding strong healths
Fatherhood of mothers
Brothers, sisters, others

Alex eternal pure love
My music tunes your rhyme
Subconscious sublime
Paper planes of crime

ISLAND WARS

Angels of crush
Solidarity of female
X y z ge-male
Both parents surviving

Hidden jungle
Deep oceans
Truly deep rest
Lost souls unrest

Allow me to feel
How calm and still
Death may be sweet
Surviving is fun

Surfing atrocities
Digital allegories
Algorithms sweet pain
Put up with the drain

Intelligence is war
Territory of swore
Be good left in the sore
Waves will heal

Misty bliss of islands
Trees of roots
Heavy boots
Paths and crossways

Difficult scary gossips
Stories of your memory
Psychology of war
Fighting me in my inbox

Clauses and applauses
Coding of my lyricism
The great Al was powerful
Emotions of possessions

Artistic liberations
Bodies and real sculptures
Life as in on stage
Outrageous games

Allow to exit
Your doors are friends
Slamming the sun
Feminine ban

Ministries of love and peace
Gathering feast
Taxation is teaching
Money be preaching

Spirits to heal
Your own gear
Tempo of wisdom
Unite your kingdom

Temples of joy
Ruffle like toy
Pray for sensation
Ally's affections

HNO

Deliberations
Underwear sensations
Waterfalls of joy
Life is a toy

If you break it
Ain't awake it
Sleeping is the beauty
Eternal sunshine loopy

Somewhere did I read
Gigantic stars won't make it
I wait till you explode
Redemption to foresee

I used to love you truly
Genuinely I was yours
Until you didn't feel it
Believe it and foresee it

Breaking up this toy
Through pains we grow
Next step life's ladder
Know limits feel flatter

My cave is craving
Furtive gardens to enjoy
Roll over misty grasses
Musical arises

Deliberate I stand
Resolving all stunts
Theater of emotion
Tender true devotion

LIFE

I want to die
Please don't cry
Jumping of the window
Makes you a true widow

Your skin's sensations
Allow you liberations
Release rivers of joy
Come on simply enjoy

Waiting in the line
Crossing borders
Countries alienations
Journeys complications

Until you run now faster
Escape life's disaster
Humanitarian misery
Dramas triggery

Starvation is stagnation
Pray for segregation
Woman's alluration
Allow me freedom

Redeem kingdom
Moon shines above molly
Tragedy of life
Survive for lust

KEDROS TREE

Roots of wisdom
Unified kingdom
Flight mode we drive
This is how we thrive

Allow us ambivalences
To find consequences
A life full of bliss
Eternal sunshine kiss

Who's gonna read your fear
Come on this is your gear
Faces of strangers
Blurry changes

What happened and you crushed
Double aged lash
Living high as a kite
Your home designate

Where you want to reside
Misery's tribe
Allure make new start
Talk about it it's hard

POWER

None of my business
Your own wizz ness
Air to fly
In peace to hide

Allow me wings
All I want is she sings
Calm and tranquility
Equilibrium trinity

Birds giving rhythm
Friendship of freedom
Unite kingdom
Pure wisdom

Love is open
Gates are swollen
Throats of wolves
Choir of trues

Hearts of unity
Galaxy of purity
I find You strong
I knew it all time long

SUMMER NIGHT

Allow em tears
Purify all fears
Truly open gears
Head honey showers
Sticky hours
Poetry's fate
Having full plate
Caress the dove
Be above
Singing lullabies
Others tragedies
Arrive in peace
Truly bliss

WINTER'S NIGHT

The movie was great
Then my clothes were out
Your kiss was dancing
All over my neck

Layers of protection
Unfolding affection
careful touch
Entering crouch

Asking for it
Slow and deep
Reach that point
That makes me numb

Unlock the joy
My body shakes
Your river flows
My veins overflooding

Round my legs
Your arms are holding
Pressure unfolds
Paradise arriving

Hugging lust
Pumping heart
Release trust
Hugging lust

SIMON & CO.

Feeling that energy
While crawling
Passing over abdomens
Explosive spirit

Emotions uncaged
Out of the box I find you
Crawling again
Scapula rubbing
Passing over your thighs

Respectful dance
Intimate touch
Choreo of life
Knocked on your shoulder

Who could imagine
Tip of the earth
Crossed points
Tight arms Lifting up
Careful not to drop

Passion arises
Jealousy of one's else
4 years of that bless

To finally understand
Opinions matter
Differ and scatter

Open explain, remain
Next move comes forward
Push yourself

Easily slide
Weaseled to Joy
Chip in enjoy

Trusting the flow
This ride ain't a sprint
A marathon is life

YVE(S)

Particles of lust
Science of dust
Madness of caress
Tender chess

Attraction like in atoms
Electrons plus and minus
Who gave you all this trust
Teaching sexual must

Funding my oblivion
Million of stars
Ecliptic as I stand
Your arms of crush

Tilting of my pointes
Dancing out all fears
Rich joy saves the boy
Running around with deers

Closing all cycles
Endless ruffles
Oblivion to seek
Peace to redeem

Axial shines denial
Geometry of freedom
Sun is your kingdom
Galaxy of pieces

Joining all misses
Lovers to remember
In pains to surrender
Life was a game

Mastering with no aim

YVE(S) VOL.2

Erections clay
Double sway
Countries crossing
Blooming glossing

Your house of wonder
Little ponder
Holy Motors
Killing donors

Shower all pain
Resurrect your drain
Somewhere did I read
Sensation is prim

Courtesy of wisdom
Unite your kingdom
Duality of fear
Madness your gear

Earth is calling
Explore this falling
Redeem liberations
Free of all calculations

Science religion
Marriage of plants
Biology plans
Magical stunts

YVE(S) VOL.3

Your lips are haunting
My area is dawning
Kisses you blow
Beautiful glow

I wonder the flow
Why can't we move
Together in dance
Enjoying the trance

In bed you jump
I follow the hump
Together in dance
Enjoying the trance

Transmission of energy
Emission of love
Devotion of fear
Forever gear

My brain connects
Your soul erects
How you, dig into love
Deep feelings on top

You know how to make
My soul cry out
All lust of trust
Sensual crush

The spot you found
To make me crown
Of fantasies and memories
Enslave beautifully

Erotic symphony
No war of gender
Just feel it splendid
I sing it, spell on

Magic of love
Atoms of microns
Connecting bodies
Exploding fountains

Mountains of peace
Beloved seas

PAUL

You the king of waves
Poseidon's wild raves
Riding with full grace
Musicals main face

Missing your deep soul
Handsome wise owl
Exploding of emotion
Exploring with devotion

Style your last name
Cute panda has no drain
Fusion white dove
Surrender avec love

Universal sweet kiss
Gentle small bliss
Authentic intuition
Pleasure for submission

Success is your caress
No needed any stress
Vibrating lust and growth
Expanding ohne loath

TANZENDER 1. MAI

Cheap stocks
Cold socks
Floor of fire
Legs desire

Blazing sun
Dancing on skin
Felt like apocalypse
Synthesizing light

My pores of wisdom
Belong to your kingdom
Memories of lust
Future of trust

Clinical research
Elevated reach
Turn around and bleach
Your past belongs to hitch

Hike your present
Uphill up-jive
Your life's beautiful tribe
Learning to leave

What no longer serves the king

HEART CHOR RAP

Dynamics are not easy
You can't be always cheesy
Surrender to the process
You won't get any losses

Bring all the beaches out
Tonight the stage is open
We gonna burn them down
All sorrows yet not spoken

So doo whatever you need
Scream it out shake your feet
Steam it tight aaall night
After darkness comes the light

To shine above your soul
Unite deeper within your core
Solutions to embrace
Confusions to erase

SUMMER HOUSE

Counting waves
On edges pledge
Arriving home
Seaside dome

Counting waves
Hearing the moon
Whispering soon

Songs of September
Never ending chamber
Paradise around you

Silver light bathing
Waters craving
Deep and shallow dreams

What you redeem
Allow me to know
Cause only true flow
Can purely glow

BATHING

I saw you
Underwater horizon
Light blue ozone
Endless white silk

Stepping on earth's cheek
Eloquent touch
Waters lash
Hugging my skin

Falling redeem
Sands castles
Underwater horizon
Light blue ozone

ECONOMICS

Adam's Smith
Invisible hand
Visible slap
Crisis alert

Free markets flirt
Eradicating faith
Fraud and mortgages
Cleaning packages

Of stocks and affairs
Capital labor land
Crisis at hand
Stringent reality

Implications Complications
Capitalism sensations
Rationality of failure
Deeply allure

Humans alienation
Laissez-faire
Markets unfair
Nudged to work best

Keynesian bless
Ricardo's kiss
Little miss
Studying economies

61

Anthropological isotopies

PERIOD

Alienation equals salvation
Systems liberation
Delirium of pain
Mother's aim

Life to give
Shiver and thrill
Delirium of pain
Mother's aim

Sensation at last
Bleeding trust
Eternal lust
Unstoppable crash

Pulsations alert
Alive I stand
Adults return
Childhood caress

KARMA

Scareless
Tune in your soul
Elaborate your goal
Psychiatrists may ask you

Keep acting cool
Delirium of fantasies
Dare to play
New life sunshine ray

Drinks and drinks
Ambrosias sins
Nectar is dripping
Her legs be shifting

Enjoy the ride
Marathon may be
Pleasure and pain
Peaceful drain

Comedy your pills
Kicking in thrills
Red in your veins
Emotions your gains

Sensation wake up
War is calling
Answer is anger
Devotion and love

Destiny's trip
Genes heal
Connection through music
Feel, amuse, lay back

Became all his
Property of wisdom
Unite your kingdom
Teams to grasp

Dionysiac lust
Groups at last
Communities attack
Souls distract

Until you elevate
Talent of the closet
Open up, light in your shatters
It's you now who matters

LIGHT & SHADOW

Your touch
My chests lust
Fire under the skin
Volcanos bright colors

Im luring up your spirit
Im lingering to hear it
I want to endure
Heavens to ensure

Your kiss is approaching
My body is now crouching
Skins left alone to dance
Passion in trance

Projections on the wall
Scenes of the past
Hunting us at last
Escaping now together

Its us who choose
Which movie each time
To play is a ray
Let the sun come in

Its us who choose
Which movie to play
Each time is a ray
Let the sun come in

Shadows to elude
Clarity now nude
Moments of caress
Keep away distress

Ride on those colors
All the shades of lust
Volcanic is the touch
Lets try a deep match

HOPE

When destiny plays games
You should definitely surrender
Mystically explain
Never again complain

Just put yourself out there
Explore the world with care
Conditions preconditions
Let em back all superstitions

Allow it all smooth flow
Make it all just blow
You deeply surely know
Spirits guard your low

To study and reflect
Till you high jump again with respect
Universal trust
Your endless lust

Travel around the globe
Ensuring all the hope
Circles to engrave
History's new wave

Brake egos and tight cages
Forgive allow all rages
Freedom comes within
Traveling even in bed
At winters graceful in

CONTENT

I dreamt long views
Through tunnels
To the sea

Breeze hushing
Colors crushing
My heart gazing still

Pleasing myself
Hidden sun
Closed curtains

Views of others
Of us ain't affect me
Their eyes even caress me

Waking up feeling joy
In content I rest
Deeply learning my test

ANDREJ

Very busy emotionally
Truly cautiously
Great news for your creation
Publikums adoration

Innocent break
Children's crave
For love and affection
Emotions liberation

Secrets to unveil
Systems to reveal
Core of fragile wisdom
Hurted red kingdom

Closed gates
Trumpets whistle
Miniature relations
Pleasures revelation

Skins communicate
Music recreate
Ecstasy of birth
Orgasms church

Dome of holly giving
Kids baptized swimming
Endless sea our fornication
Blessed courses of iteration

GROWING

Rhythm of flow
Chartering glow
Surrender and blow
Sun is better with snow

Advisor becoming
Operations vermeiding
Building up trust
Enjoying pure lust

Discovering where
Leading with care
Crisis redeem
Managing the unseen

Deliberations to wish
Strategies to twist
Resolving is kingdom
Traveling is wisdom

Drama is to feel
Climax to seek
Learning on deep
Ecstatic redeem

It's all open said
Now is time to be shared
Knowledge is power
Growing every hour

Stillness to witness
First time date
Situations crave
How beauty exists

Solitudes bliss
Smiling at ease
Accepting hardness
Caressing harness

It hurts cause you grow
Remember life's flow
Enjoying has tears
Erase all fears

Colorful pains
Journeys drains
Ain't play with statistics
Riding luck's lyrics

Education your seed
Emotion your bleed
Your water be it love
Pumping air at heart's dove

PROCESS

Angels on earth
Flowers ahead
Gratitudes pledge
Thank you for existing

Expand to grow
Contracts soul
Push me up
Remind me low

Forgot to bow
Live your flow
Clapping is time stopping
Surrender gods are laughing

Above and beyond
Not always fond
Question the pond
Come out straight on

Dry your body's frown
Before you jump in
Again pleasures deem
Pause and reflect

Bias suspect
Unlearn what you learn
Wake up concern
Closer to come

Arriving at feelings
Admitting all needing
Admire your trust
Live up your lust

JESPER

The smell of freedom
All over your spirit

The taste of excitement
All over your lips

The sense of humor
All over your words

The young child
Against all dogma

Voice of the blues
Dressed up in peace

Gray figured eyes
Northern smile

Scared face corners
My fingers climb

Your skin soft invites
Surrender to us

Energy floating
Inside exploding

Light fireworks
Sattle Sparks

Gazing deep calm
Gentle little punk

EPICTETUS

Everybody gonna hurt you
So will you do too
Question is if they do
Due to human dynamics

Or they real motherfuckers
Question wide open
Blowing your mind
Redem what is fine

Answer the riddle
Choose the Divine
Control of let go
Energy of beaux

Futile to spend
Powers to those
Ain't change ain't move
The way you choose

Past is your treasure
Memories pleasure
Haunting pains
Unsolved drains

Carrying them now
Choosing the how
What to let go
Which battle to gift

Universe's lift
Courage to change
What should cranes
take away with fly

Your present is power
Standing up your tower
Gazing your choices
Stop living in doses

STARDUST FLOW

Rhythm and blues
I learned from the booze
Solely embrace
Life's rootspace

Rhythm and poetry
I felt it through floetry
Cathartic the flow
Emotions that grow

Coming up as alive
Visualizations
Your deeper sensations
Allowing is trust

Enjoying is lust
Break down the crust
Ain't you wait to last
Bathing now in stardust

KEATON'S WORLD

Visual storyteller
Emotions seller
Queen of seduction
Self abduction

Cards ain't deemed
Communicate only
Actions are holly
Grale foreseen

Each gesture unique
Found out the sleek
Audience asleep
Wake up a squeak

Finding the angle
Perspective angel
Trying and error
Admitting no terror

Observing the life
Cameras placements
Graceful statements
Landscape of strife

Each frame a painting
Long lasting graining
Seeds retaining
Flourishing maintaining

Sustainable lust
No random crush
Connection of stardust
Cosmic colorful trust

HAPPY NAME DAY

Brain and body
In the fight
Who's being
Now more light

Victory to seek
Balance to feed
Who's gonna win
Pulling in the wind

Yesterday my brain
Whispered in the rain
Hey body I surrender
You won this render

Flexibility in mind
New reality will shine
Signs to unveil
Paths being surreal

Taking them is life
Slowing down the fight
No reason now to rush
Allow yourself to flush

Red flowers on the grave
Beauty on the name
The grand grand mother smiles
Passes you her name

Identity to rise
AnaSTARsia no lies
Values to restructure
Life your new culture

Fear to overcome
Love to overdone
Yourself the first player
Honesty your new layer

CHARM'S

Living angel
Caribbean babe
Breeze of the south
Promise land's fire

Eyes of the sea
Horizon of blue
Love at first
Passion's caress

Crossed paths
In Berlin's lust
Beauty is the day
I met you in a ray

Of sunshine and joy
Salutations am Feld
Secret fest
Hugging rest

Winters blankets
Cozy dance avec you
Waiting the summer
To shine next to you

Happy birthday my love
Pure Health for
The body mind and soul
Full of surprises
Positive arises
Your growth in all levels
Our celebration in heavens

FEMALE & VICTOR

Brains connect
Unconscious I want you
Tropical of cancer
My soul was a dancer

Fire jumping lions
Draw me all your crayons
Paint me the future
My fantasies await

Your rich sensations
Rivers of affection
My veins overflooded
Pumping heart no fears

Authentic as I laugh
My souls subtract
Primitive pleasure
Worries leisure

Nobody did measure
How deep you can feel
Abyss of clean waters
Moon shines above us all

Roger

I do now copy
I'm ready to explode
Your Cuban dance seduces

Reality reduces
Pure Substances of fear
Destroy all the gear

Do not allow the spin
Master your own sin

Drugging life was hell
Control your guns of horror
Work with all your sorrow

Alone we arrive
In black holes we thrive
Asteroids collapsing

Creating magicians
Your life's alchemicians
Life happens in those spots

Too

Believe it to feel it
Wake up to relief it
Progressive is your pain
Forgotten is your drain

Minimal rain
Will make you feel
Intelligence swift
True gifts are given

Forgotten on the sore
Mermaids will care
Bodyguards of her

Feminine erosion
Your power of lust
Who you should trust

CHALLENGE

Control your powers
Take care of your showers
Boarding in peace
Matching at ease

Hang the clang
At any cost
Now you are lost
Ephemeral ghost

Of memories trembling
Stories ascending
To truly exist
Amidst all bliss

Reverse counting
Only discounting
Oxytocin lasting
Hugging my lust

Deeply trust
Gut feeling crush
Due to disparities
Eternal clarities